LITTLE   THEIR BIG

KIDS & DOGS   VOLUME 2

REVODANA PUBLISHING
81 Lafayette Avenue, Sea Cliff, N.Y. 11579

ISBN: 978-1-943824-40-3

www.revodanapublishing.com

LITTLE THEIR BIG
KIDS & DOGS VOLUME 2

BY ANDY SELIVERSTOFF

REVODANA
PUBLISHING

TABLE OF CONTENTS

Here we go again!

If you already own the first volume of *Little Kids and Their Big Dogs*, then you know what's in store with this second one: Lots of gorgeous photographs of little kids kissing, cuddling, playing, laughing, jumping and just generally loving the big dogs in their lives.

My *Little Kids and Their Big Dogs* adventure started off accidentally: Some good friends asked me to set up a photo shoot with their toddler Alice, and when their huge Great Dane Sean came along, he seemed like a natural element of the shoot. Soon the special relationship between tiny Alice and her towering canine companion became the focus of the photos.

Today, thousands of photos and dozens of shoots later, there are two *Little Kids and Their Big Dogs* books, greeting cards, a calendar ... It seems people just can't get enough of these adorable kids and the big but gentle dogs they call their own.

"Aww" factor aside, another special aspect of these photos is their ability to introduce people to some unique and exceedingly rare breeds. I can't tell you how many people have told me they never knew about the dreadlocked Hungarian herder called the Komondor ("Is that a mop?") that is on the cover of the first book, and in the last chapter of this one. Also in this volume, you'll meet other dogs that are just as "undiscovered," like the Ca de Bou from Spain, the Beauceron from France and the Caucasian Shepherd from Russia.

Though they come from different parts of the world, with unique histories and functions, they share what all dogs have in common: their capacity to love the people in their lives — especially the very smallest ones.

At left: **Julia Veshkelskaya, who authored all the stories in this book and the previous one, with her Harlequin Great Dane Leonella Di Lorense.**

RAIN, RAIN, GO AWAY

The sky frowns as a warm summer rain pours down. Drops softly tap on the broad leaves of the lindens, playing a sad melody as if on piano keys.

Alla walks through the park and sings along with the rain. The park is empty — everyone has obviously decided to stay indoors on this bleak day. The girl is about ready to return home herself — her umbrella protects her from the rain, but her sneakers can't save her from the puddles — when she spies a black smudge ahead.

It turns out to be a dog. "I'm Nero Wolfe," the fascinating creature says. "I'm a Great Dane puppy."

"Puppy?" says Alla, surprised: The only puppy-like thing about Nero are his expressive, wide-open eyes. "But you're so big!"

"Mom says that I'm still very young. I'm only three months old, and soon I'll be taller than she is."

A raindrop falls on the puppy's nose, and he shakes himself awkwardly. Alla remembers her umbrella and moves closer. "My mother says I'm little, too," she offers. "Probably all mothers are like that."

Reminded of his mother, Nero looks around. Before seeing Alla, he had been distracted by a bird in a lilac bush, and now he is alone. "Don't be upset — we'll find her!" Alla reassures him.

Soon they see a Harlequin Great Dane walking back along the path. Leonella is very gracious and thanks Alla for finding her puppy, letting the girl stroke her white and black fur.

"My owner Julia still thinks I'm a baby, too," Leonella tells the two little ones as a timid ray starts peering through the thinning clouds. "All mothers *are* like that."

GENTLE WAVES

One day Deli the Poodle sees a girl on the beach. The snow-white dog often meets children on her walks, and they are always in awe of her. "What a beautiful dog!" they exclaim. "A real princess!"

Deli knows most of the little children on this stretch of coast, but she has never seen this girl before.

And for once, it's Deli who is enchanted: The girl slips along the shore in a graceful dance, lithe and light as a feather.

Deli loves to dance, too, so after admiring the girl for a long time, she decides to approach her.

"You dance very beautifully," the Poodle offers. "What do you call this dance?"

The girl, who introduced herself as Maria, shrugs her shoulders. "I don't even know," she laughs. "I just love to dance."

As Maria hums, Deli rises on her hind legs and slowly spins. Clapping, Maria begins to sing, beating out a rhythm with her hands. "Brava!" she says when Deli has finished. "Let's dance together!"

Maria shows the Poodle her dance moves, and Deli copies them perfectly. It is as if the two have known each other forever, and soon their movements meld together effortlessly, turning a set of individual dance steps into a conversation without words.

WISHING ON THE SUN

Marika hasn't seen her friend Weiss the Afghan Hound for a very long time. At their last meeting, the snowdrifts had only just begun to melt, and now the birch branches are covered with a thin lace of dainty greenery.

At first the girl is angry at her friend; then she begins to really worry about him. "Maybe he's just bored with such a little girl," her older brother teases her.

Then one day, Weiss runs up to meet her. "My owner and I went away," he explains. "I missed you!"

A wonderful day gives way to a gentle evening. Marika sits at the very edge of the water so that the boldest wave can barely touch her new shoes, and she listens to the fables that the Afghan Hound loves to tell. "I'll teach you what to do to make your dream come true," her exotic friend tells her.

Marika claps her hands, and the Afghan Hound continues. "In ancient times, people believed the sun was one of the most powerful gods," he says. "If someone makes a wish at sunset and transfers it from his hand into the hands of the sun god, he will get his wish!"

"How can you give the sun your wish if he doesn't have any hands?" Marika asks, puzzled.

Weiss smiles. "The last ray of the sun is his hands!"

The girl jumps up joyfully and spreads her hands to the horizon, where the ball of the sun is descending into the smoothness of the bay like a huge orange. "How do I know if the sun god gets my wish?" she asks. But Weiss just smiles behind his long mandarin beard.

When the sun dips into the water, Marika makes a wish and feels the heat of the last ray on her palms. She laughs happily. "Now I'm sure my wish will come true!"

SPEED RACERS

Tyra and Makadara the Rhodesian Ridgebacks are natural competitors.

"I'm the first to catch the ball!" Makadara shouts when they play with their little owner Vasilisa.

"No, I run faster!" Tyra protests, overtaking her friend.

Vasilisa is both amused and upset, because the dogs compete for her attention, too. They push each other out of the way when she pets them, and they keep count of who gets more caresses.

One day when Tyra and Makadara start to argue again, Vasilisa throws up her hands and exclaims, "You are just like my friends the twins. You're always arguing with each other!" But then Vasilisa remembers that those twin brothers don't quarrel when they compete against someone else.

Inspired, Vasilisa climbs into the toy car she got for her birthday. The two Ridgebacks crowd around, arguing about who gets the passenger seat.

"I can't take anyone," the girl says. "And this goes very fast." She strokes the steering wheel.

"It's no big deal," Makadara sniffs. "We run faster!" Tyra frowns. "I bet Makadara and I will be the first to reach those trees!"

The engine growls, and the little car peels off. The Ridgebacks rush ahead of Vasilisa, who purposely slows down so the dogs finish first.

"We won!" Tyra jumps up, hugging Makadar, who laughs in response: "No car can beat us!"

Then they sit on the grass and have a picnic. And for the first time in a long time, the Ridgebacks don't argue.

SLAM DUNK

Milana offers an apple to her friend Grace. The Giant Schnauzer thanks her, but doesn't eat it. "I prefer cookies," Grace mutters indistinctively because of the apple in her mouth.

"I love them, too, but my mother says I have to eat my fruits and vegetables," Milana explains. "Proper nutrition and sports are very important for a healthy lifestyle!"

Grace cocks her eyebrow. "Sports?"

"Yes. That's when you walk for a long time, and run and jump."

Grace chomps the apple in her mouth. "You know, I think sports are a little different than what you're talking about. Sports are things like football, volleyball, swimming and running."

"I like basketball," Milana says. "If I play basketball, does that mean I'm doing sports?"

Grace nods, and they walk in silence for a while. "But you have to be in good shape to play basketball, or any other sport," Grace says finally. "For example, I go to dog shows, and my handler and I run around the ring. It looks easy, but the preparation took a very long time."

"Grace, you're a professional," the girl concludes. "Could you help me to learn a sport?"

Grace is pleased at the idea of being a coach. And so every morning, Milana and her Giant Schnauzer friend run around the park, do morning exercises and then play ball — a small but cheerful basketball team.

SOME BUNNY

"Let's play!" Arina says to Mitch, her Ca de Bou. "You, me and Bunny!"

The girl picks up her favorite stuffed-rabbit toy. "And," she announces, "now I'm a Bunny, too."

But as they walk along the street, Arina's spirits suddenly deflate. "Everybody who walks by mentions the pretty little girl with her beautiful dog!" she cries. "Nobody calls me Bunny!"

Mitch looks at Arina, then at Bunny, and then at the girl again. His kind has been developed in Spain to catch bulls, but these days the only things he tackles are Arina's every desire. "Hmm … Let's try to think logically," he ponders. "Why doesn't anyone understand that you're a Bunny?"

"A bunny is smaller than I am?" Arina volunteers.

Mitch shakes his massive head. "No … A cat is small, too, but you can't mistake it for a Bunny."

Anna considers that for a moment. "Oh, I understand," she says brightly. "A Bunny has long ears!"

"Ears — exactly!" Mitch thinks for a moment. "I know what we need! I'll be right back!" Minutes later, he is running up the path, holding something in his teeth. "Put it on," he tells the girl as he tosses a hat into her lap. "It's a magic hat!"

Arina twirls it in her hands, immediately noticing the long, soft ears. "Now I have the right ears," she reasons, "and anyone can understand that I'm a Bunny!" As if to confirm her words, a passerby calls out, "What a wonderful Bunny walking her dog!"

Mitch puffs his chest up. He couldn't be prouder of himself for solving the Bunny crisis. "Let's go — I'll show you a whole meadow of dandelions," he announces. Arina claps her hands, and two Bunnies and one Ca de Bou run to look at a field blanketed in yellow.

BULLY FOR YOU

One day, Yaromir returns from school to find his smiling parents waiting for him in the entrance hall.

"You have been asking for a dog for a long time, son," his dad says, opening the door to the living room. "Meet the newest member of our family!"

Out of the room comes a little fawn-colored blur, with huge, clumsy paws. The boy throws his backpack on the floor, exchanging it for the puppy. "A Bullmastiff — that's what I've been dreaming about!" Yaromir cries. "His name is Lucky because he is my greatest piece of luck ever!"

His parents laugh, and then his father says seriously, "Son, you need to remember that Lucky is not a toy. You'll have to take care of him, feed and walk him. Lucky is small now, but he'll become very big!"

Yaromir promises his parents he will take care of Lucky, and he is true to his word. He cleans up after him, walks him, and takes him to the vet for his vaccinations and wellness checks. The boy happily gets up an hour earlier in the morning to feed and exercise his puppy, and in the evenings he walks Lucky for a long time, even though he is tired from school and homework.

On weekends, Yaromir and Lucky go to training class, and the boy is always very proud because Lucky is the smartest and most obedient dog in the group.

Within a year, the small puppy has grown into a huge but incredibly well-mannered Bullmastiff — and a neighborhood favorite.

"Luck had nothing to do with how well your dog has turned out," Yaromir's father tells him with pride. "It's all because of your hard work!"

INNER PUPPY

Uma the Cane Corso is a serious lady. She always walks sedately beside her owners, dignified and reserved, scanning her surroundings for any sign of danger or trouble.

But Uma can't help but turn into a playful puppy when children come into view.

And there is one child in particular whom Uma loves. She met him when friends of her owners came to visit, bringing along someone so small he was her same height — she was only a puppy herself back then.

Uma cautiously approached the boy and sniffed him. Delighted, Ratmir hugged her, and looked into her eyes with his own wide ones.

When Uma ran into the other room, all the adults laughed, thinking the baby had scared her. But she returned carrying a favorite toy that she never, ever shared with anyone, and laid it at the little boy's feet.

Years have passed. The boy has grown up, and so has the Cane Corso. Every weekend she waits impatiently for Sunday, when these same friends and their son Ratmir often join them for a walk together.

The boy and the dog run around and come up with new games. Although Ratmir has grown up quite a bit, to Uma he remains the same baby that she met on that long-ago day when she relinquished her very best toy. And whenever she sees him, inside Uma is her puppy self, all over again.

PIXIE PATROL

"Morgan, do you believe that fairies exist?" Keegan the Irish Wolfhound asks his older friend.

"You'll be a year old soon and you still believe in fairy tales?" Morgan sighs. "Of course there are no fairies."

Their little owner Ivan vehemently protests. "They do exist! I know it for sure!"

Morgan knows that Ivan believes in Santa Claus and expects an invitation from Hogwarts when he turns eleven, so the senior Wolfhound only shakes his head in response. But Keegan keeps insisting. "We'll prove it to you by showing you the fairy." He runs ahead, then turns off the main path onto a narrow, grassy one.

When a gap of light appears between the tree trunks, Keegan slows down and whispers, "Shhh! Don't frighten her away!" A little girl sits in a small clearing. Sunlight flashs through her wheat-colored curls. Ivan thinks she isn't as small as a typical fairy, but she seems much more charming than the ones he's read about.

Trying not to frighten the girl, Keegan carefully draws closer and sits down next to her. "Hello, fairy!" he says, but she only laughs. "I'm not a fairy. My name is Agatha." She says that she sometimes walks there because she loves the woods so much. "I help the flowers to wake up," Agatha says, stroking her hand along the grass.

On the way home, Morgan is uncharacteristically cheerful. "Agatha is a wonderful girl!" he tells Keegan. "Of course, you were wrong about her being a fairy, but I'm very glad we met her!"

"Never mind, cranky old Morgan," Ivan thinks. "Keegan was absolutely right." The boy had seen the white flower buds open in the green grass as if by magic, as the tiny fingers of a fairy named Agatha caressed them.

A WRINKLE IN TIME

Katyusha poses the question to her fellow Neapolitan Mastiff: "What if we had a boy at home?"

Alik looks incredulously at his wrinkled, gray friend.

"The kids in our house grew up a long time ago. Now they live far away and only visit once in a while," Katyusha explains, her furrows of skin jiggling as they walk. "Our owners work now. Children are ready to play and hug all the time. And I love it so much when someone scratches my belly."

"Where do we get this boy?" her friend demands.

"They say they can be found in the forest," Katyusha ventures.

Alik snorts. "Don't be ridiculous! We're walking in the park!"

Dejected, Katyusha lowers her head so that her face is even more wrinkled than usual.

Then, at the turn of the path, they glimpse Max. His family moved recently from another part of the city, and he sees the two Mastini — that's what they're called back in their native Italy — walking there regularly. "Sometimes I play alone because my friends have other things to do," he explains.

The Mastini offer to walk with him, and soon they are playing and running. But when it is time for Max to return home, a tear runs along the rope of skin that hangs from the corner of Katyusha's eye.

"Don't be sad," Alik comforts her. "Max promised to come with his friends tomorrow! And they'll all pet and play with you!"

Katyusha's eyes gleam again — but this time with happiness, at the idea of little boys and girls being as plentiful as her many wrinkles.

PHOTO FINISH

The Central Asian Shepherd Dog named Matal begins this morning as she usually does: She walks around the yard checking to see if there are any other tracks on the freshly fallen snow, and if the gate is closed. Then she returns to the house, wakes up her owner's grandson, little Arijus, and leads him to the bathroom to brush his teeth and wash.

At breakfast, the boy's grandmother says they are going to have their photograph taken together.

"What about Matal?" Arijus jumps off the chair and hugs the dog. "I'll only be photographed with her!" The dog wags her tail and licks the boy's warm palm.

After a night-long snowfall, all the lawns, roads, sidewalks and roofs have been painted white, making it look like a fairy town of powdered sugar. As they walk, all the passersby respectfully make way for the little boy and the Central Asian Shepherd who is walking beside him.

Arijus is impatient to get to the center of the park, where the photographer is waiting for them, but the old dog walks slowly and the boy adjusts to her pace. Matal tries to go faster, but they have been walking for a long time, and she is tired.

As he had insisted at the breakfast table, Arijus is photographed with just the dog. Matal is happy to see the smile on his face.

"Maybe I don't run as fast as I used to, or jump as high, or play as long," the nine-year-old dog thinks to herself. "But I definitely know that I can always make Arijus smile!"

STOP THE PRESSES

When Leon grows up, he wants to be a journalist. He interviews and photographs his mom and dad, and all his friends and neighbors.

"Soon you'll get the Pulitzer Prize!" his dad tells him. "Only the best journalists get that award!"

Then, on a visit to his grandparents in the countryside, the boy sees his most exciting subject yet: a huge red Tibetan Mastiff that looks just like a lion. As he approaches the house, Leon strides very purposefully, clutching his camera. At the gate is the huge dog.

The Tibetan Mastiff stares into the boy's eyes. "I'm Gromila," he says, then slowly turns away.

Leon doesn't know what to do. A dog who looks so sad can't be angry, so he sits down next to Gromila and asks what is wrong.

"When my owners have visitors, the little people play with me," the Tibetan Mastiff sighs. "But there haven't been any guests for so long. And the neighbors are all afraid of me."

"I'll play with you!" Leon offers, getting to his feet just as the dog does. "After that I'll interview you!"

Delighted, the mastiff tells Leon all about his majestic ancestry, about about how the wind howls as it rushes across the Tibetan plateau, and how delicious yak milk tastes.

That evening, Leon hugs Gromila, digging into the dog's thick, red coat. "I'll write an article about how kind you are," he promises. "People will read it and stop being afraid of you. You'll have a lot of new friends!"

The Tibetan Mastiff breaks into a broad smile. Leon is grinning, too. Never mind a Pulitzer — the real prize is such a wonderful new friend!

BECKONING SPRING

"Baggy, do you know what day it is today?" asks little Alexandra, who wears a fur coat and her favorite fluffy shawl that her grandmother knitted for her.

Baggy the Caucasian Shepherd Dog waits patiently for the answer as the girl fastens the sled to his harness.

"A long time ago, when even my grandmother's grandmother was not born, people saw off the winter. It was one of the most joyful holidays," Alexandra explains excitedly as Baggy navigates through snowdrifts. "To make sure winter was definitely gone, people sang a song. My grandmother sang it to me, but I forgot the words and now spring won't come ..."

"Don't be upset!" Baggy says, turning around and winking. "We'll chase the winter away!"

At the edge of the forest, the girl sees a shiny samovar perched on the stump of an old fallen tree, steam rising from its lid. "Your grandmother and I wanted to surprise you!" Baggy says affectionately as the girl arranges the teacups, one for each of them.

On the way home, Alexandra is so happy that she begins to sing softly. "I remember!" she exclaims.

> *Burn brightly,*
> *Do not go out!*
> *Look at the sky: The birds are flying,*
> *The bells are ringing!*

The snow crunches under Baggy's footpads. A light frost nips the girl's pink cheeks. But the air is already smelling of spring.

EASEL DOES IT

One day Butch meets a girl on a walk. She is very small and sits right on the path. "My name is Marusya. I'm sitting here because I am very upset," she sobs.

Like any mastiff, Butch is a very thorough dog. His kind evolved in Spain, where they protect sheep from wolves and other intruders. Little girls are even more precious than sheep.

"Well, first of all, take a seat on the park bench," Butch tells her. "You'll freeze sitting on the ground, and I'm uncomfortable listening to you all the way down there — you're too small and I have to bend."

Marusya does not want to move, but the Spanish Mastiff seems nice, so she sits down on the bench and tells her story. The teacher at her school has asked the children to draw a dog over the weekend. Marusya is doing her best, but nothing seems to go right.

"I came to the park especially for that," Marusya continues. "There are a lot of dogs walking around, but they run all the time and they won't stand still long enough for me to draw any of them!"

"I know how to solve your problem," Butch says. "I'll sit down and won't move until you draw me!"

Butch's portrait turns out so well that the teacher wants to hang it in the most prominent place in the classroom, but Marusya won't let her.

"I just brought it to show you," she explains. "It's my friend Butch. When he comes to visit me, he'll be so happy to see his portrait in my room!"

ALL GROWN UP

"Katya, please, I'd like to walk Elbrus by myself," Mashenka says to her older sister. "I'm already grown up — I dress myself, I clean my own room, I even can cook breakfast myself!"

Katya watches with a smile as Elbrus the gangly Mastiff puppy plays with a ball. "Being grown up isn't just about making breakfast," she tells her sister. "It means taking care of someone besides yourself, like Elbrus. He needs to learn to listen to you, to understand what you want from him."

"Like you do with Atti?" Mashenka asks, nodding at the grown-up Mastiff who listens attentively to the conversation from his stately perch on the sofa. "I can do that, too!"

True to her promise, every day Mashenka gets up an hour early. She copies everything her sister does, scooping kibble into a bowl and making sure Elbrus' other bowl has fresh water at all times. Mashenka teaches Elbrus to come when she calls him and to obey if she tells him to leave something.

One day Mashenka runs to her sister and whispers, "Katya, you know, Elbrus brought me a ball and said that he wanted to play! I heard every word!"

"Why are you whispering?" her sister asks with laugh. "You did everything right and now you have learned to understand Elbrus. In fact, Atti talks to me all the time."

Elbrus nods and grumbles. "It's about time — I thought that little girl would never hear me!" For emphasis, he scratches his ear loudly with his paw. Mashenka's eyes widen in surprise and Katya laughs again.

The next morning, everyone goes to the park: Katya walks her full-size Mastiff Atti, and little grown-up Mashenka leads the puppy Elbrus all by herself.

FRIEND AT FIRST SIGHT

It's getting colder. The September sky is covered with a thick blanket of clouds that won't get around to raining.

Lisa and her two Leonberger friends walk slowly through the park. The girl doesn't feel like playing tag, and even the dogs are in a dreamy mood. They all sense the cold rain and shorter days starting to close in.

"Look! That's the first person we've seen today," Michael the Leonberger says, nodding at the approaching figure. The trio has fallen into the habit of guessing who they will meet first on their regular walk. Today both dogs think that the grandmother with the fluffy Pomeranian will be the first one they spot; Lisa says that it could be her neighbor with the two Chihuahuas because they left their house right after she did.

But this time none of them guesses right. It is a boy, almost the same age as Lisa. He greets the girl pleasantly, then turns to the dogs: "Hello! My name is Arthur."

Lisa offers her name, as do Prosha and Michael the Leonbergers. "I've never seen such big and beautiful dogs in my life," the boy exclaims, and he listens with interest as Lisa tells him about them: As their name hints, these huge, hairy dogs originated in Leonberg, Germany, and in the 1800s they were considered the ultimate companion for royalty around the globe. Every duke and princess and nobleman wanted one, because they were prized not just for their good looks, but their gentle, unflappable temperaments.

The Leonbergers listen approvingly, and the new quartet walks on as if they have been friends forever.

"Who do you think we'll see first?" Lisa asks. "Maybe, Prosha, you'll be right about the grandmother and her Pomeranian!"

STAGE SET

There are only a few days left before the dog show. Mary and her two Beaucerons are going to prance around the ring in front of a judge, but not in the usual way: They are enrolled in a doggie-dancing competition.

Mary has carefully taught Ayda and Arvin to offer their paws, dance on their hind legs and roll over. Both dogs have all the choreography down pat, perfectly anticipating her cues.

In the backyard, Mary turns on the tape recorder, and they complete the entire dance routine twice — perfect both times. "Now all we need to do is wait for the weekend!" she exclaims. "The show will be held in a huge hall, and there will be plenty of spectators."

Arvin rushes around happily, but Ayda stands at a distance, barely wagging her tail. "She's afraid she'll forget something," Arvin whispers to Mary, "and everyone will think she's stupid."

Mary smiles, sits next to Ayda, and hugs her. "What you are feeling right now is called 'stage fright,'" she explains. "It goes away after the first performance. Arvin and I, we were very scared at first, too. But I'll tell you the same thing I told Arvin: No matter what happens, ribbons or not, you are both still the best!"

The Beaucerons begin to lick Mary's face. "I have an idea," she laughs. "Tomorrow we'll call all our friends and neighbors, gather as many people as possible, and show them our dance routine. Then it will be easier to cope with Ayda's stage fright.

"And now," she concludes, picking up the dogs' favorite toy, a flying disc, from the grass, "let's play!"

DREAMTIME

During the day, Marika watches a television program about Borzoi. That evening, as she drifts off to sleep, she remembers the graceful Russian Wolfhounds racing ahead of hunters dressed in traditional costumes, and they follow her into her dreams.

Marika walks a gravel path through a well-groomed estate. Three Borzoi — Marselle, Yalta and Olympia — lounge in the shade of a terrace, their aristocratic heads resting on their paws.

Spotting her, the dogs vault over the marble steps in one jump. Marika pats their silky hair. "You should be taken for a walk now. The guests will arrive soon and they will hunt with you tomorrow."

Marselle nods. "We are waiting for one now." Marika grimaces: She dislikes that gentleman-hunter. He knows the value of Borzoi and always tries to persuade her father to sell him one of the dogs. The man likes Olympia the best, but Marika's father would never sell her, nor Yalta. The previous time this unpleasant gentleman almost convinced Father to sell Marselle — or so Marika thinks.

As Marika plays with her Borzoi friends, they hear a clatter of hooves: His Excellency has arrived.

Taking Marselle by the collar, Marika heads to a lodge on the far shore of the lake. Unused for a long time, it is the children's favorite hiding place. But that doesn't prevent adults from knowing about it.

"I will never sell our Marselle to anyone!" Marika's father laughs when he finds her there hours later. As for the unwelcome interloper, "we agreed that when there are puppies, he will buy one."

Satisfied, Marika clasps her father's hand and hugs Marselle.

A bright sunbeam touches Marika's closed eyelids, and wakes her up. "No big deal," she thinks contentedly, stretching. "I'll visit them again in my next dream!"

BEACH DAY

Alexandra likes to visit her mother's friends near the shore, not least of all because her dear friend Hard the Akita lives there.

One early winter evening, as snowflakes circle outside the window and logs crackle in the fireplace. the girl looks into the fire and says, "I miss summer a lot."

The Akita yawns and shrugs. "I prefer winter – it's too hot in the summer." The girl tousles his head tenderly. "Of course, you have such thick fur you don't feel the cold!"

When the long-awaited summer comes, Alexandra remembers that conversation. Hard is fond of walking, but she sees he is uncomfortable on hot days. "Hard, do you like the sea?" she asks.

"Just a lot of water," he shrugs.

"Let's go to the beach today," she suggests, and finally Hard nods in agreement.

Hard is impressed by splashing through the water: It's a lot of fun, and so cool he doesn't even notice the heat. Besides, Alexandra is happy, and that makes the Akita happy, too.

When the day is almost over, the girl and her friend admire the soft June sunset.

"You liked the beach," Alexandra says, guessing his thoughts. The ocean is quiet, flecks of the passing day dancing on its surface. The Akita smiles and looks into the girl's eyes. "I like summer now, too!"

NOTHING TO SNEEZE AT

When Michael appears in the house as its newest and smallest family member, Gerald the Golden Retriever isn't jealous. Not one bit. But he is worried — very worried, to be sure.

In the yard next door is a huge, shaggy dog. Before he arrived there a year ago, he lived with another owner who had gotten him as a very small little puppy. They lived happily for a long time, until the new baby arrived, and became allergic. One raw spring morning the dog's owners drove him to the other side of town — and left him behind.

"What does this allergy look like?" Gerald asks as soon as Michael arrives home.

"Well, their cheeks turn red," his friend answers.

Every morning, Gerald runs up to the baby's room and checks his cheeks. Day and night, month after month, he repeats the ritual, so distracted he doesn't notice how little Michael has grown to love him.

The baby grows up, learns to sit, then to walk, and the Golden Retriever is there to help steady him. Michael plays and the dog brings him toys, the baby falls asleep and Gerald lies down next to his crib. "Gerald" is the boy's first word.

Gerald forgets all about the allergy. Once, on a family walk, a woman stops to talk to the boy's mother and mentions she has never gotten a dog for her children because she worries they might become allergic.

"Our Gerald is the best nanny for Michael!" his owner replies, embracing her son with one hand and stroking their proud Golden Retriever with the other.

FUZZY MEMORIES

Baydush the Komondor waits patiently as her owner blow-dries her dreadlocks.

"Well," her mistress says, "now you're as good as new for your photo session tomorrow."

"What do I have to do?" the Hungarian sheepdog asks dubiously.

"They will tell you," her owner assures her. "And you'll be with a professional model who has already done photo shoots with Komondors."

Baydush often has her photo taken, sometimes with passersby who want a memento of such a rare breed. Still, she is nervous: This is her first time participating in a photo shoot with a very well-known photographer (her owner talks about him!) and a professional model, no less ...

The next morning Baydush and her owner arrive at the park at the appointed hour, but find only a lady with her young son. "Hello!" the boy says with a smile. "I'm Arthur. Do you want to play?"

Baydush looks inquiringly at her owner, who nods. Arthur is a cheerful companion, and after a few minutes Baydush completely forgets why they have come to the park.

"Oh, it's time for me to go!" she exclaims when she sees the tall man with the camera. "We have a photo session. Do you see that photographer? A model is coming and then we'll shoot!"

Arthur smiles modestly. "I'm the model. And our photographer has already taken a bunch of shots."

Baydush steps back, contemplating the boy. "What should we do now?" she asks, looking back at the photographer.

Arthur laughs and calls to her. "Come on — let's play!"

ABOUT THE PHOTOGRAPHER

More than 25 years ago, a long-haired Saint Bernard came into Andy Seliverstoff's life, and things were never quite the same again. Because dogs never live as long as we want them to, Andy eventually found himself without an industrial-sized mound of fur at his feet. That's when the first Great Dane arrived at his family's home in Saint Petersburg, Russia — and he's had one ever since.

The dogs also led Andy to his career as a professional dog photographer. For the last decade, he has been a fixture at major dog shows throughout Russia and Europe, where he photographs big-winning show dogs and the people who love them.

The main goal of Andy's *Little Kids and Their Big Dogs* photo shoots is not just to create beautiful pictures, but to capture and transmit the state of endless joy and mutual confidence between the children and the animals. And in the end, Andy hopes all his photos convey this important message: Love for dogs and children makes people kinder.

Revodana Publishing published Andy's first book, *Little Kids and Their Big Dogs*, in early 2017 to critical acclaim from the likes of People magazine ("Outrageously precious"), the Today show ("Nothing short of magical") and Buzzfeed ("You'll never see anything as adorable"). This book is the second volume of an ongoing series. Also available is a stunning calendar featuring images from both books, as well as a new line of greeting cards.

For updates on Andy and his ongoing *Little Kids and Their Big Dogs* project, please visit www.littlekidsbigdogs.com.

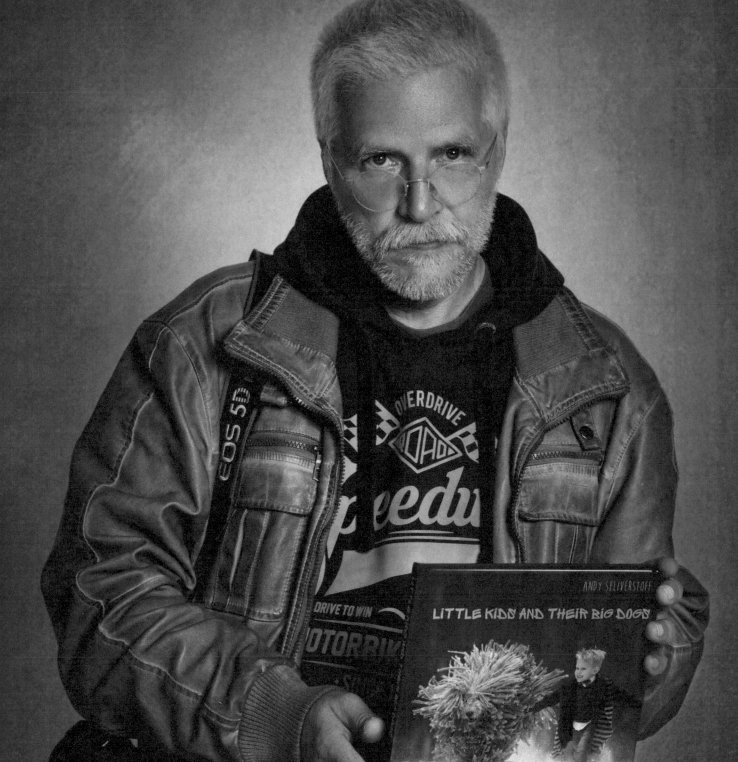

MORE BOOKS BY REVODANA PUBLISHING

Little Kids and Their Big Dogs: Volume 1

The Leonberger: A Comprehensive Guide to the Lion King of Breeds

Everyone's Guide to the Bullmastiff

The Official Book of the Neapolitan Mastiff

The Afghan Hound: Interviews with the Breed Pioneers

The Best of Babbie: The Wicked Wisdom of Babbie Tongren,
the Afghan Hound's Sharpest Wit

Your Rhodesian Ridgeback Puppy: The Ultimate Guide to
Finding, Rearing and Appreciating the Best Companion Dog in the World

Canadian Inuit Dog: Icon of Canada's North

ESPECIALLY FOR CHILDREN

Peyton Goes to the Dog Show

How the Rhodesian Ridgeback Got Its Ridge

VISIT WWW.REVODANAPUBLISHING.COM

CPSIA information can be obtained
at www.ICGtesting.com
Printed in the USA
LVHW070245030119
602434LV00002B/11/P